THE ST. LOUIS CARDINALS

Sloan MacRae

PowerKiDS press.

New York

Published in 2012 by The Rosen Publishing Group, Inc.
29 East 21st Street, New York, NY 10010

First Edition

Editor: Amelie von Zumbusch
Book Design: Greg Tucker
Layout Design: Ashley Drago

Photo Credits: Cover (background), p. 7 Joe Robbins/Getty Images; cover (Albert Pujols), p. 22 (bottom) Scott Boehm/Getty Images; cover (Stan Musial), pp. 13, 22 (middle) Photofile/MLB Photos via Getty Images; cover (Bob Gibson), p. 15 Bruce Bennett Studios/Getty Images; p. 5 Mitchell Layton/Getty Images; p. 9 Chicago History Museum/Getty Images; p. 11 Hulton Archive/Getty Images; p. 17 Ronald C. Modra/Sports Imagery/Getty Images; p. 19 Robert Caplin/Bloomberg via Getty Images; p. 21 Dilip Vishwanat/Getty Images; p. 22 (top) Mark Rucker/Transcendental Graphics/Getty Images.

Library of Congress Cataloging-in-Publication Data

MacRae, Sloan.
  The St. Louis Cardinals / by Sloan MacRae. — 1st ed.
      p. cm. — (America's greatest teams)
  Includes index.
  ISBN 978-1-4488-5009-9 (library binding) — ISBN 978-1-4488-5151-5 (pbk.) —
ISBN 978-1-4488-5152-2 (6-pack)
  1. St. Louis Cardinals (Baseball team)—History—Juvenile literature. I. Title.
  GV875.S74M33 2012
  796.357'640977866—dc22
                                      2011000157

Manufactured in the United States of America

CPSIA Compliance Information: Batch #WS11PK: For Further Information contact Rosen Publishing, New York, New York at 1-800-237-9932

CONTENTS

THE NATIONAL LEAGUE'S BEST

The St. Louis Cardinals are one of America's best baseball teams. **Major League Baseball** is formed by two big groups, called **leagues**. These are the American League and the National League. Every year the top teams from each league play each other in the **World Series**. This is baseball's **championship**. The Cardinals have won the World Series more times than any other team in their league.

Many fans agree that the Cardinals are the best National League team of all time. They have won the most **pennants** and the most World Series championships. In fact, only one other **professional** baseball team has more wins than the Cardinals.

Over the years, the Cardinals have had great players, such as Chris Carpenter. Carpenter joined the Cardinals in 2004.

THE CARDS

The Cardinals play in St. Louis, Missouri. This city sits where the Missouri River flows into the Mississippi River. The Cardinals play in a ballpark called Busch **Stadium**. Thousands of Cardinals fans pack Busch Stadium for every home Cardinals game. Some fans call the team by nicknames, such as the Cards and the Redbirds. Cardinals are red birds, after all!

One of the team's **logos** is a picture of a cardinal sitting on a baseball bat. Another logo shows the letters *S*, *T*, and *L*, which stand for "St. Louis." The Cardinals are big **rivals** of the Chicago Cubs. Cardinals fans love it when their team beats the Cubs.

Busch Stadium opened in 2006. You can see St. Louis landmarks, such as the Gateway Arch, from the stadium.

THE BROWN STOCKINGS

Baseball is an old sport. It has changed a lot over the years. The Cardinals have changed with the game. For one thing, they were not always called the Cardinals. The team we now know as the Cardinals began as the Brown Stockings, in the 1880s. They were called this because they wore brown socks. People soon began to call them the Browns.

Then, the Browns changed their colors to include red. It no longer made sense to call them the Browns. For a short time, they were known as the Perfectos. In 1900, they became known as the Cardinals. They have kept that name ever since.

Homer Smoot was one of the Cardinals' top hitters in the early 1900s. He played for the team from 1902 until 1906. Smoot was nicknamed Doc.

THE GASHOUSE GANG

The great **slugger** Rogers Hornsby joined the Cardinals in 1915. He was one of the best hitters ever. It takes more than great hitters to win championships, though. With that in mind, the Cardinals hired Branch Rickey as **manager**. Rickey's top skill was finding great young ballplayers and turning them into stars. One of these groups became known as the Gashouse Gang in the 1930s.

The Gashouse Gang was known for having fun and being silly during games. They were also known for winning. Two of the best Gashouse Gang players were brothers named Paul and Dizzy Dean. The Gashouse Gang won the World Series in 1934.

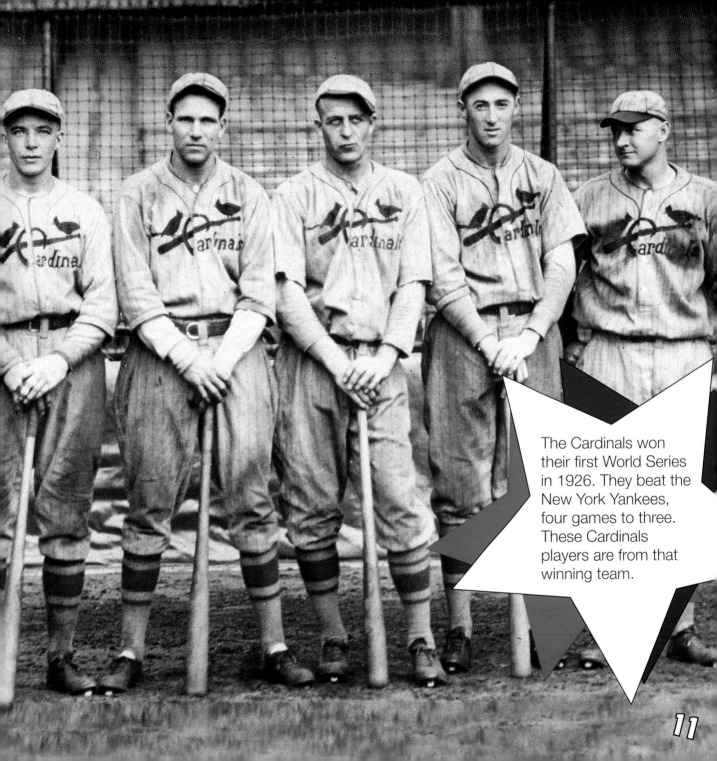

The Cardinals won their first World Series in 1926. They beat the New York Yankees, four games to three. These Cardinals players are from that winning team.

STAN THE MAN

Baseball history was made again in 1941 when Stan Musial took the field for the Cardinals. Fans at the time likely had no idea that Musial would spend 22 seasons as the Cardinals' star player. Musial was nicknamed Stan the Man. He became one of the biggest names in all of American sports. He set several records and helped the Cards reach the World Series in 1942, 1943, 1944, and 1946. They won championships in three out of those four World Series appearances.

Stan the Man continued to lead the Cardinals through the 1950s. However, it would take new players to get St. Louis back to the World Series.

Stan Musial led the National League in batting in seven different years. He was named the league's MVP, or most valuable player, three times.

BOB GIBSON

Stan Musial played his final game in 1963. By then, it was time for new Cardinals leaders. Star players such as Bob Gibson and Tim McCarver became those leaders. They led the Cards to win the World Series in 1964 and 1967. Gibson was one of the best **pitchers** in baseball in 1968. That year St. Louis reached the World Series again. Not even the Cardinals can win them all, though. St. Louis lost the championship that year to the Detroit Tigers.

The Cardinals had been the best National League team for a long time. Now they struggled, though. The Redbirds failed to win a pennant in the 1970s.

Bob Gibson set a World Series record in 1968 by striking out 17 players in a game. He also threw 13 shutouts, or games in which no player scored, that year.

WHITEYBALL

In the 1980s, a new manager once again led the Cardinals to greatness. Whitey Herzog joined the team in 1980. Herzog got his players to play the game faster. The Cardinals were soon called the Runnin' Redbirds. Their fast style of play became known as Whiteyball. Herzog and the Cardinals won three National League pennants with the help of star players such as Darrell Porter, Ozzie Smith, and Willie McGee. In 1982, they won the World Series again.

The great Tony La Russa became the Cards' manager in 1996. He led the team to more great seasons. In 1998, Mark McGwire broke the season **home run** record.

Ozzie Smith played shortstop for the Cardinals. He was a great defensive player. This means he played really well in the field, when the other team was up at bat.

ALBERT PUJOLS

A young hitter named Albert Pujols joined the Cardinals in 2001. He quickly earned a spot in baseball history. He became one of baseball's hottest stars in a very short time. Pitchers from other teams hated throwing to him.

Pujols led the Cardinals to the World Series in 2004. However, St. Louis lost to the Boston Red Sox. They fought back two years later and reached the World Series again in 2006. Baseball fans across America did not think the 2006 Cardinals were good enough to win the championship. Pujols and the Cards proved them wrong by winning a tenth World Series for St. Louis.

Here, team members celebrate after the Cardinals won the 2006 World Series. The Cardinals beat the Tigers, four games to one.

A LEAGUE OF THEIR OWN

Many teams never win a pennant. They never even get to play in the World Series. The Cardinals have won more pennants and more World Series championships than any other team in the National League. Their players, managers, and leaders have changed the game of baseball forever.

The Cardinals have been so good for so long that they have fans not only in St. Louis. The Cardinals have fans all over the world. Stars like Yadier Molina and Chris Carpenter will keep the Cardinals on top of both the National League and the baseball world for many years to come.

The Cardinals have lots of fans, both young and old. Cardinals star Albert Pujols signed a baseball for this young fan in 2009.

21

ST. LOUIS CARDINALS TIMELINE

1900
The team takes the field for the first time as the St. Louis Cardinals.

1922
Rogers Hornsby wins the first of his two Triple Crown Awards for being the best hitter in baseball.

1941
Stan Musial plays his first game for the Cardinals.

1934
The Gashouse Gang beats the Detroit Tigers in the World Series.

1963
Musial, now a grandfather, gets two hits in his final baseball game.

1964
The Cardinals beat the Yankees in the World Series.

1982
The Runnin' Redbirds beat the Milwaukee Brewers in the World Series.

2009
Albert Pujols is named the National League's most valuable player for the third time.

1980
Whitey Herzog manages his first game for the Cardinals.

GLOSSARY

CHAMPIONSHIP (CHAM-pee-un-ship) A contest held to determine the best, or the winner.

HOME RUN (HOHM RUN) A hit in which the batter touches all the bases and scores a run.

LEAGUES (LEEGZ) Groups of sports teams.

LOGOS (LOH-gohz) Pictures, words, or letters that stand for a team or company.

MAJOR LEAGUE BASEBALL (MAY-jur LEEG BAYS-bawl) The top group of baseball teams in the United States.

MANAGER (MA-nih-jer) The person in charge of the players and coaches on a baseball team.

PENNANTS (PEH-nunts) League championships.

PITCHERS (PIH-cherz) Players who throw the ball for people to hit in baseball.

PROFESSIONAL (pruh-FESH-nul) Having players who are paid.

RIVALS (RY-vulz) Two people or groups who try to get or to do the same thing as each other.

SLUGGER (SLUH-ger) A baseball player who hits well.

STADIUM (STAY-dee-um) A place where sports are played.

WORLD SERIES (WURLD SEER-eez) A group of games in which the two best baseball teams play against each other.

INDEX

WEB SITES

Due to the changing nature of Internet links, PowerKids Press has developed an online list of Web sites related to the subject of this book. This site is updated regularly. Please use this link to access the list:
www.powerkidslinks.com/agt/cardinal/